ROMNEY HYTHE & DYMCHURCH RAILWAY

ANDY STANSFIELD

HALSGROVE

First published in Great Britain in 2008

Copyright © Andy Stansfield 2008

British Library Cataloguing-in-Publication Data
A CIP record for this title is available from the British Library

ISBN 978 1 84114 729 1

HALSGROVE
Halsgrove House,
Ryelands Industrial Estate,
Bagley Road, Wellington, Somerset TA21 9PZ
Tel: 01823 653777 Fax: 01823 216796
email: sales@halsgrove.com
website: www.halsgrove.com

Printed and bound by D'Auria Industrie Grafiche, Italy

Dedicated to the memories of

Kevin Crouch and Suzanne Martin

who lost their lives on 3 August 2003 and 10 July 2005 respectively
in separate locomotive accidents on the Romney Hythe & Dymchurch Railway.

Between them they gave over 35 years service to RHDR.

INTRODUCTION

This delightful 15 inch narrow-gauge line runs from the Cinque Port of Hythe for 13½ miles to the shingle spit of Dungeness with its fishermen's cottages, lighthouse and nuclear power station, taking in four other stations along the way. These are the small seaside town of Dymchurch, St Mary's Bay, New Romney where the RHDR is based, and Romney Sands.

It owes its origin to three people in particular: Captain JEP Howey, Count Louis Zborowski and Henry Greenly. Howey and Zborowski were both wealthy and fascinated by miniature railways, and Greenly was the engineer who was chosen to design the locomotives themselves. The Count and Captain Howey were also motor racing enthusiasts, a passion which was to lead to Zborowski's premature death in the Italian Grand Prix before the RHDR was even open to the public.

With their eyes on the famous Ravenglass and Eskdale Railway, they went ahead with the design and construction of the first two locomotives but their hopes of purchasing the Lake District line were dashed. However, Greenly suggested Romney Marsh as an alternative possibility. So it was that, on 16 July 1927, the RHDR opened with track which stretched from Hythe to New Romney via Dymchurch. It was another year before the additional track was added, extending the line to Dungeness.

The line survived the ups and downs of the depressed thirties, the Second World War, post-war recovery and beyond but by the time Howey passed away new investment was sorely needed. A succession of owners followed but it wasn't until Sir William MacAlpine and a group of financial backers took over the line in 1973 that sufficient investment was made to return the line and its facilities to former glory.

Today the tireless work of dedicated volunteers is responsible for its success, generation following generation in some cases. The Romney, Hythe and Dymchurch Railway Association works as a preservation society, its members regularly forming working parties to ensure the upkeep of the line and sharing their boundless enthusiasm with visitors from all over the globe who, for eighty years, have enjoyed both spectacle and a childlike sense of fun.

In total there are eleven steam locomotives and two diesels; each are both named and numbered, with numbers running from one to fourteen (there is no thirteen). It is rare that, at any one time, all will be serviceable. During the preparation for this book Green Goddess (No.1), The Bug (No.4), Hurricane (No.8) and the diesel John Sutherland

(No.12) were all out of action. Doctor Syn (No.10) was on light duties and Southern Maid (No.3) was in the workshops some of the time having a big end replaced.

Several of the locos have given pleasure to members of the Royal Family in years gone by. Northern Chief carried the Duke of York during the line's first official engagement on the occasion of his visit on 5 August 1926, almost a year before the line opened to the public. The official opening took place the following year on 16 July 1927 when Hercules hauled the inaugural train from Hythe to New Romney. Thirty years later Hurricane hauled a royal train carrying The Queen, the Duke of Edinburgh, Prince Charles and Princess Anne and to commemorate this event Hurricane now carries a plaque on the side of its cab.

The history of individual locos is quite fascinating, The Bug being a good example. The first RHDR loco to be designed by someone other than Henry Greenly, she was constructed in Germany and was intended primarily for use during the construction of the line. After its completion she was sold to a Blackpool showman and changed hands twice before being consigned for scrap in 1950. Amazingly she survived intact, unused and unloved, for just over twenty years and came to the attention of Sir William MacAlpine who acquired her and had her returned to New Romney for extensive restoration. Since then she has delighted countless young children by serving in her capacity as Thomas The Tank Engine and on Santa Specials.

Also not to be missed is the Model Railway Exhibition situated upstairs above the buffet at New Romney, head-quarters of the RHDR, where visitors will also find the engine sheds and workshops. The model exhibition is an 00-gauge layout surrounded by historic photos of the line's development. The models are computer-controlled and include a wide variety from passenger trains to freight, covering Europe-wide railways from the last hundred years with stations, turntables, water towers and crossings all meticulously laid out. For more information on this and other aspects of the Romney, Hythe & Dymchurch Railway you can visit their website at www.rhdr.org.uk

The station car parks are filled variously with shiny new 4x4s and elderly saloons with a dent or two to add character – and that variety is significant. Perhaps it's an obscure benefit of the RHDR, but it brings together people from all walks of life and that is no bad thing in this day and age. Young and old, wealthy and not so wealthy, people come to look, to reminisce, to smile and most importantly they leave with a spring in their step.

Andy Stansfield

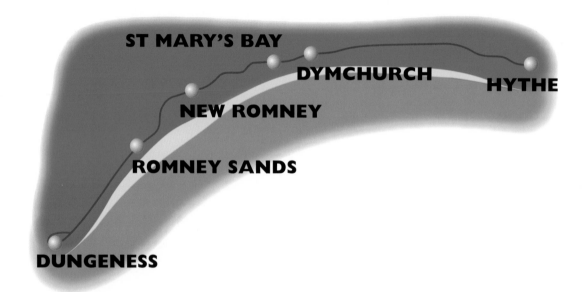

ST MARY'S BAY

DYMCHURCH

HYTHE

NEW ROMNEY

ROMNEY SANDS

DUNGENESS

Romney Hythe & Dymchurch Railway: stations map

No.9 Winston Churchill

When commissioning this locomotive Howey, who favoured Canadian Pacific designs anyway,
specified a Canadian-style cab to give better protection from the British weather.

Tender

Asking a driver what he carries in his tender is a bit like asking a businessman what he carries in his briefcase apart from sandwiches, but mostly it comes down to rags and oil.

When I grow up. . .
George and Oliver Stevens from
Ashford, aged seven and four
respectively, have few doubts about
what they would like to be when they
grow up and are pictured here with
driver Mike Jacques who has already
achieved that ambition.

Spic and span
Driver Simon Foulkes gets No.2 Northern
Chief ready to roll, taking on water and
providing an already very clean locomotive
with a last minute polish.

Magical qualities

There's something quite powerful which tugs at my attention when photographing certain subjects, something mysterious to do with the blend of line and shape. Sometimes as I stalk a subject, photographing it from different perspectives, this mood can disappear equally quickly. Here I managed two different shots of The Bug while this force was at work.

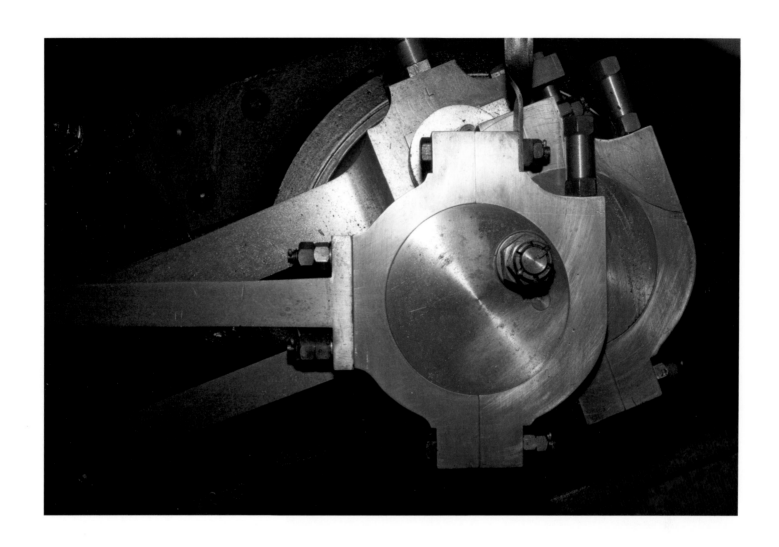

Signal box
At New Romney Station the signal box is only at the end of the platform and, if it's at all possible, a polite request for a peek inside will probably be answered positively.

St Mary's Bay

The station at St Mary's Bay is no more than a halt. The bungalow previously owned by the author of *The Railway Children* lies adjacent to the track on the right.

No.5 Hercules

Passing beneath the bridge by Romney Marsh Visitor Centre, just outside
New Romney, is Hercules on its way to Dungeness.

Signals, New Romney Station

This set of signals is probably the single-most photographed aspect of the RHDR, positioned as they are in the sun and at the north end of the platforms – a much less cluttered setting than the footbridge end. They appear in the background of so many images that I felt they deserved a photo in their own right.

Driver's eye view
This is the fairly cramped space a driver must operate in. In winter that means a cold wind around
the ears and legs toasted by the intense heat each time a shovelful of coal has to be added.

Manufacturer's plate
The Yorkshire Engine Company of Sheffield completed two Canadian Pacific-style locomotives for the RHDR:
No.9 Winston Churchill and No.10 Doctor Syn (originally named Black Prince on delivery). I use the term
'completed' because Davey Paxman started to build them and Krauss provided the boilers from Munich.

Rolling stock
A standard 16-seater closed saloon, pictured here with New Romney signal box in
the background, is part of an extensive range of rolling stock.

Signal box at Hythe

If you are fortunate enough to get a look inside the signal box at Hythe this is what you'll see. For photographers it's a challenge on a sunny day to balance the whites and reds plus the greenery outside the windows!

No.10 Doctor Syn

When built in 1931 this loco was actually named Black Prince. However in 1948 the original Doctor Syn (No.9) was shipped to Toronto for an exhibition and in a fit of post-war patriotic fervour No.9 was renamed Winston Churchill and the name Doctor Syn was applied to No.10 instead. Doctor Syn was a fictional character from local smuggling stories. The name Black Prince (first applied to No.10) was then re-allocated to No.11 when it was acquired in 1976.

No.4 The Bug
Sadly this children's favourite, which doubles as Thomas the Tank Engine for a few days each year, was confined to the New Romney workshops during my various visits.

St Mary's Bay

One side of St Mary's Bay Station is backed by fields and it's possible to obtain a
wide variety of photographs without any distracting background.

Isolated detail

There are lots of opportunities around the locos and the different stations to isolate detail. In some cases the outcome can be rather abstract whereas other subjects are more immediately recognisable.

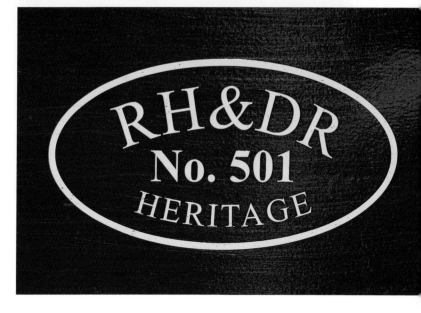

No.5 Hercules at St Mary's Bay

This shot demonstrates one of the major problems of taking photographs along the RHDR: by and large it runs north-south which limits opportunities to get the sun behind you. For the technically minded, this is a composite of five different exposures using high dynamic range and tone-mapping software.

No.5 Hercules with large capacity tender

Following an accident in August 2003, Hercules was withdrawn from service and sent for
a complete overhaul, returning to service in May 2005 sporting a new Midland Railway red livery
along with a large capacity tender. The latter was first fitted after the Second World War
when Hercules was rebuilt following wartime duty as an armoured train.

No.9 Winston Churchill

In 1973 the Winston Churchill was converted to an oil-firing loco as an experiment. After a successful trial it was restored to its conventional configuration due to the rising price of oil.

All change!
Winston Churchill is one of RHDR's locomotives which has changed colour over the decades.
It was painted red for an exhibition in Canada in 1948 and then black in 1962 but now
sports a red livery reminiscent of the London Midland and Scottish Railway.

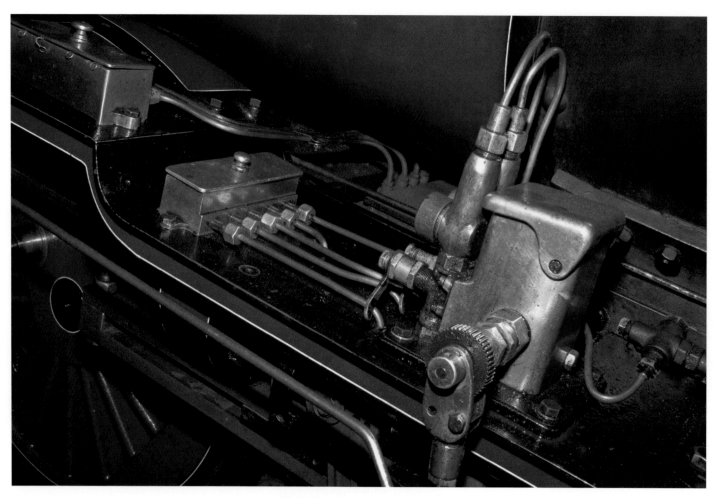

No.3 Southern Maid detail

This was another locomotive undergoing an overhaul during my first visit and it gave
me a chance to get up close and personal with some of her fine engineering.

No.3 Southern Maid manufacturer's plate

A two-cylinder 4-6-2 Pacific weighing in at 8½ tons, Southern Maid was designed
by Henry Greenly and built by Davey Paxman in 1926–1927.

No.2 Northern Chief detail
It's always tempting to include the complete engine but there are times when there is
too much going on in the background and a more selective approach works better.

New Romney workshops

Another patient receiving treatment in the workshops during my visits was No.6 Samson. Originally built to operate commercially carrying ballast along the line, Samson had great difficulty negotiating the early points and crossings and between 1931 and 1946 remained unused except to be raided for spare parts.

No.11 Black Prince
The distinctive smoke deflectors help to identify Black Prince, pictured here at
Dymchurch Station with the memorial garden in the background.

No.5 Hercules entering Dungeness Station

There is no turntable at Dungeness. The line enters the station on a broad curve which sweeps through the station and beyond, eventually bringing it back on a northerly heading once more for the return leg towards Hythe. This curve makes Dungeness the most flexible location for obtaining photos with the sun in an agreeable position.

St Mary's Bay

Pictured here at St Mary's Bay Station before departing northwards to Hythe, No.9 Winston Churchill
is about to cross one of the most pastoral stretches of the line.

No.14 Captain Howey

After leaving the outskirts of New Romney on the northward trip to Hythe, trains pass a golf course on the right just before the line ducks beneath the road bridge adjacent to the Romney Marsh Visitor Centre. It is possible to park at the Centre and learn a little more about this fascinating area as well as capturing a few train photos.

Memories are made of this!
This is another example of the type of close-up detail which is worth recording. For me at least, just the name Castrol is highly evocative. I can't read the word without recalling the aroma of oil burned off by the racing motorcycles I used to watch most weekends in my youth.

Mind the gap!

When photographing, or even just admiring, locomotives in the station it's as well to remember to leave a little distance between yourself and the engine because sharp bursts of steam like this can lead to an unpleasant surprise.

RHDR Engine Drivers

Opposite: Simon Foulkes lavishes care on his regular ride, No.2 Northern Chief.
Above: No.6 Samson with volunteer driver Tim Gray.
Right: No.3 Southern Maid is dwarfed by driver Robert Featherstone.

No.6 Samson

Samson's black livery was exchanged for red in preparation for its 1984 appearance at the
Garden Festival in Liverpool. After another paint job in 1989 the colour scheme was changed
to dark blue, similar to that of the former Great Eastern Region, but some bright red touches remain.

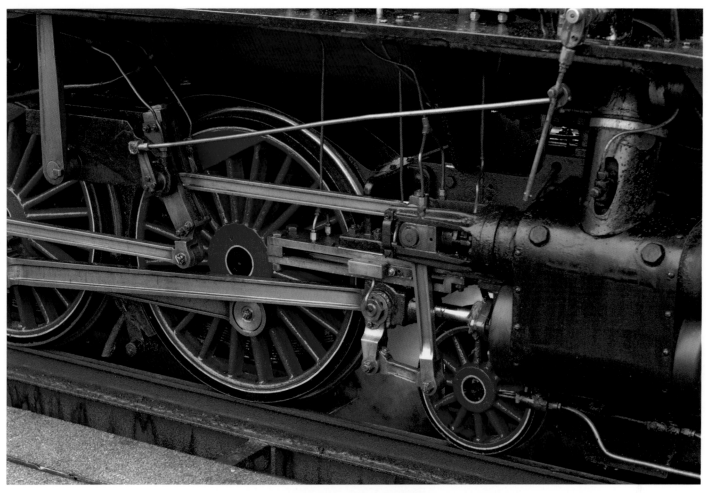

New Romney turntable
It is nowhere near as attractive as the one at Hythe, but the turntable at New Romney does allow much closer access and the possibility of some close-up shots.

From a Chief to a Maid
No.3 Southern Maid was originally intended to be named Southern Chief but at the last minute
Captain Howey changed his mind and this was changed to Southern Maid.

Opposite: No.2 Northern Chief
There aren't many wooded stretches along the line and this shot was taken by a narrow
belt of woodland between New Romney and Romney Sands, reached by driving to the end
of the narrow lane which starts by the parish church in New Romney.

New Romney workshops

Ian Dawes, pictured here welding, is typical of a number of RHDR employees. As a child he was involved with the line from 1975 because his step-father, Charlie Farrow, worked for RHDR from 1975–2002, having previously worked for British Rail. Charlie worked on electronics and signals and was very involved with upgrading the level crossing lights. Ian himself has worked as a plate-layer and driver and now works solely as an engineer. He has worked for the line for twelve of the last twenty four years and solidly since 1994. Also pictured here, rather dramatically suspended in chains, is No.3 Southern Maid. Completely stripped in the same workshop was No.12 John Southland, a 6-cylinder Perkins diesel locomotive built in 1983, which was out of service throughout the period this book was being prepared.

New Romney Station
Dark clouds gather to the north of New Romney but all the carriages used
by RHDR provide at least moderate shelter in case it rains.

Black and white
Some images, such as this shot of the Winston Churchill in full steam as it enters
New Romney Station, work fabulously when converted to black and white.
Unfortunately the monochrome version of this shot would be out of keeping with the book!

Brew time
The train schedules are organised
so that drivers get the chance of a
quick break and a brew at New
Romney before continuing their
journey to Hythe or Dungeness.

Double-header days

The RHDR periodically organises double-header days when two engines provide the pulling power for a particular service. These are always the subject of some excitement and, because of the number of possible permutations, they provide the enthusiastic photographer with the chance of a more unusual picture.

Morning chores

During the hour or so before services start to run from New Romney, its coal yard is visited by a succession of drivers in order to load up with coal. It's fascinating to observe the different facial expressions of drivers as they carry out this particularly dusty task.

Signal box at New Romney
Bright and cheerful, simply designed, and very accessible: the signal box
is very much part of the station complex at New Romney.

Saturated colour

What attracted me to this shot, taken in the New Romney workshops, wasn't so much the interesting shape of the coupling but the vivid colour which is given its intensity here because I used flash to light the subject.

Approaching Dungeness

A great deal of the area around Dungeness is protected in one way or another, as a Site of Special Scientific Interest or as a Nature Reserve. The protection around the nuclear power station, however, comes in the form of armed police officers. I had to get permission from the Head of Security to wander around taking photos, just in case they thought a long lens on a tripod was something more menacing!

A variety of coaches
In the foreground is a standard luggage saloon in Oxford blue, behind which is an open
saloon and in the distance standard 16-seater closed saloons also in Oxford blue livery.

Mixed feelings

Chatting with these passengers from across the track, this happy family snap of mum, dad and the boys waiting at Dymchurch Station actually sees them sitting by the memorial garden for Kevin Crouch, a driver killed in a level crossing accident in August 2003.

No.7 Typhoon entering Dymchurch Station from Hythe

Dymchurch is extremely popular with holidaymakers. The passengers carried by Typhoon will disembark here to make their way back to their caravan holiday home or to drift off to some of Dymchurch's tourist attractions.

No.3 Southern Maid
Most of the drivers look the part, with faded denims imbued with just the right
amount of coal dust, a peaked not-quite-black cap and a red neckerchief.

Dungeness
The station at Dungeness is set against a strange backdrop of fishermen's wooden chalets,
an old and a new lighthouse, and the sheer bulk of Dungeness nuclear power station.

Dymchurch
Opportunities for a different vantage point are always welcome. Dymchurch Station has a useful footbridge which provides a great viewpoint looking north towards Hythe.

Next stop Romney Sands
No.6 Samson at New Romney
waiting to depart southbound for
Romney Sands and Dungeness. The
lack of light beneath the station roof
can be a nuisance, photographically
speaking, but it does help the
steam to stand out.

New Romney turntable
No.10 Doctor Syn being given a spin, quite literally, by volunteer driver Roger Prince, previously a full-time driver for four years who now only works peak season and normally drives No.5 Hercules.

No.6 Samson nameplate

As well as usually being marked with its individual number, each locomotive carries a nameplate.
In this case the nameplate is crescent-shaped and positioned along the side of the loco.

Opposite: No.11 Black Prince

Black Prince ready to lead a double-header from New Romney to Hythe. This loco is more
easily recognised by the lack of a number on its buffer bar. It was one of three locomotives built by
the German manufacturer Krupp in 1937 for a trade fair held in Dusseldorf.

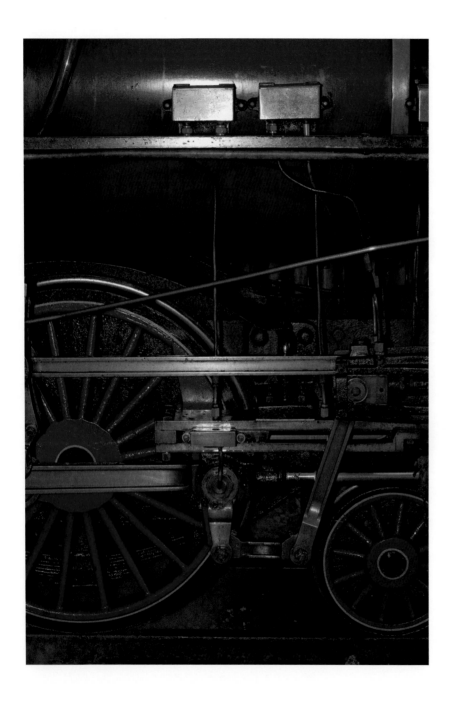

No.9 Winston Churchill detail
While long shots of the locomotives perhaps have the most romantic feel, the engineering detail is equally fascinating. The effect is always enhanced by the presence of steam.

Emerging from the shadows
No.10 Doctor Syn passing New Romney
signal box. It is generally accepted that
this locomotive is nearing the end of its
life and its inclusion in the schedules
tends to be spasmodic.

Taking on water
The sun lights this scene beautifully, with steam set against the dark background of the trees.

Opposite: I know it's in there somewhere!
No.9 Winston Churchill at St Mary's Bay Station before departing northwards to Hythe.

KEEP
CROSSING
CLEAR

BOTOLPH'S BRIDGE
CROSSING
TO CONTACT
RAILWAY
phone
01797 364062

No.5 Hercules
This image was taken at one of the updated level crossings between Hythe and Dymchurch.
The effect was achieved by using a slow exposure with the camera mounted on a tripod so that the
crossing itself is rendered sharp and the only blur is that of the locomotive. The trickiest part was
timing the exposure so that I captured the flashing lights!

Simple arithmetic

Eleven and three make – no, not fourteen – a double-header comprising No.11 Black Prince at the front and No.3 Southern Maid ready to depart New Romney for Hythe. Provided no other train is standing at the adjacent platform, it's easy enough to capture both engines at this end of the station.

Warm work
The author was privileged to share Northern Chief's cab from St Mary's Bay to Hythe one day, an opportunity only possible under normal circumstances on driver training days. It was a bit of a squeeze but it enabled me to get a few shots that would have been impossible otherwise, though the bumpy ride meant that it was impossible to avoid some camera shake!

Set of points
The points which were fitted in the early days of the RHDR later had to
be changed as some of the locos had difficulty negotiating them.

No.7 Typhoon at Dungeness
The Typhoon's smoke deflectors were only fitted in 1955. Three years
later it was also fitted with a superheated boiler.

All aboard!
The green flag is alive and well and still in use at New Romney, Dymchurch, Dungeness and Hythe.
At Romney Sands and St Mary's Bay the driver is responsible for ensuring that passengers have boarded.

Opposite: Rolling stock at Dungeness
In the foreground is Marjorie, in a fetching mix (depending on your tastes) of brown and cream. Beyond
her is a teak composite luggage/saloon and a mix of open and closed teak saloons. The restoration of the
teak-bodied coaches has been ongoing for several years. Each is stripped down to the bare wood, timber
replaced where necessary, then stained and given multiple coats of varnish.

Maker's nameplate
Nameplates like this one from Davey Paxman serve as a reminder that these engines have seen
far more history than the vast majority of passengers and spectators.

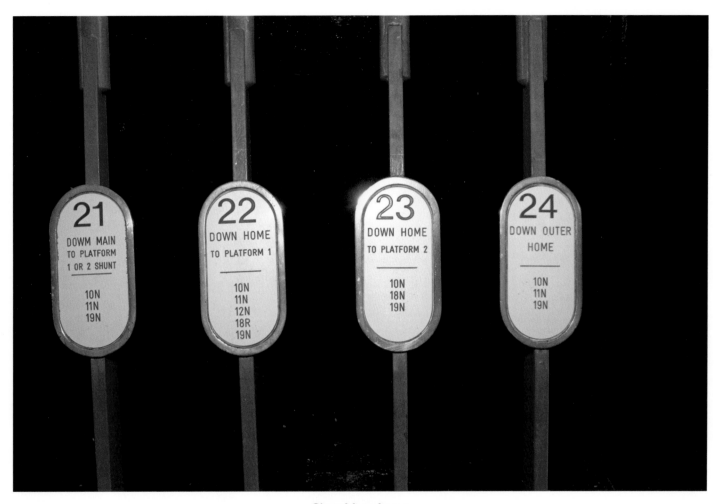

Signal box levers
All the levers are clearly marked with the signals they operate.

Approaching Hythe
Eager faces line the platform as their train pulls into the station. This engine will be uncoupled
and another will take the train to Dungeness.

Opposite: Time to reflect
Whilst passengers and spectators are generally enjoying themselves in a relaxed fashion,
the drivers have to keep to a fairly relentless schedule during peak season, so a few moments
of relaxation while waiting for other factors to fall into place are always welcome.

No.14 Captain Howey
This diesel, named after one of the
line's two founders, is shown here
approaching St Mary's Bay Station
from Hythe. At the far end of the
southbound platform this wonderful
hawthorn overhangs the track,
framing the oncoming loco.

Warning signs

Despite the fact that carriages carry signs warning passengers not to lean out of the windows or doors, boundless enthusiasm often takes over. The only danger this eager child was in was from a trackside photographer but that might not have been the case.

Model railway exhibition

Above the restaurant at New Romney can be found RHDR's fabulous model railway exhibition. A wide variety of landscapes and track configurations complete with tunnels, working signals, sidings, a turntable and even a mountain railway are computer controlled. At any one time there may be as many as a couple of dozen trains running.

Approaching Dungeness
Crossing a sea of shingle, No.2 Northern Chief approaches Dungeness through a landscape which, so I'm told,
is officially classified as 'desert' due to the very limited range of plants which will grow there.

Opposite: No.11 Black Prince entering Dungeness Station
The open setting of the station at Dungeness provides plenty of scope for photographing both engines
and rolling stock, but there is always an inescapable background of telephone wires.

No.7 Typhoon detail
This is one of my favourite close-ups and was shot in the workshops at New Romney. It was very dark and the lighting comes from bouncing flash off the wall behind me. The wall was coated by decades of smoke and I'm surprised it reflected any light at all.

Opposite: a different view of the same subject.

Hythe turntable

I couldn't have wished for better light to capture the vivid spectacle of Hythe turntable in action. Two men can swing an 8½ ton locomotive through 180° in a few minutes. Both the setting and the turntable itself offer the photographer far more scope than the considerably less attractive one at New Romney.

Sense of identity
The RHDR logo can be seen here, built into this set of signals. Surprisingly, perhaps, it doesn't feature as prominently at the stations as one might expect.

Upgraded level crossing

This is one of the level crossings which has been modernised in recent years,
about to be traversed by No.14 Captain Howey.

No.3 Southern Maid in New Romney's coal yard
First thing in the morning, a gleaming Southern Maid has just loaded up with
coal and is ready to start carrying eager passengers along the line.
The vast majority of travellers start their journey at Hythe.

St Mary's Bay

No wonder the driver is smiling: it's a glorious day and all is right with the world – but notice how exposed the driver is. Wet and windy days are a different matter altogether and it's necessary to remember that this is a year-round service.

A drop of oil always helps

Routine in-station maintenance is something the drivers can often be seen carrying out while waiting for departure time. The look of sheer concentration on the driver's face adds interest to the image and helps to focus the viewer's attention on his task.

No.9 Winston Churchill detail
New Romney Station provides lots of opportunities for shots like this but flash is necessary due to the
extensive station roof which makes the setting quite dark.

St Mary's Bay

As northbound trains enter St Mary's Bay Station they cross this barrier-less level crossing, one of a small number yet to be upgraded following two fatal accidents in recent years. On both occasions it was the engine driver who paid the ultimate price.

The old lighthouse at Dungeness

No.14 Captain Howey is pictured here leaving Dungeness with the old lighthouse in background. For a not very small fee it is possible to enter the lighthouse and climb to the very top, providing a staggering view across the shingle expanse of Dungeness.

Romney Sands Station

An embarrassing moment that's best postponed when there's a photographer around! The young man in question can be forgiven because riding around all day on wooden seats certainly does take it out on your posterior. This station serves the holiday parks which make up a large part of Romney Sands.

Limited visibility

The cab has a couple of tiny windows, one on each side facing forwards, which offer precious little sight of the track ahead. To see anything much at all, it is necessary for the driver to stand up and look over his cab roof, resulting in a face full of steam and soot – and a broader view though not necessarily a clearer one.

Marjorie
This closed saloon is often paired with traditional teak rolling stock, much of which has been recently restored.

Gladys

Named after the wife of the railway's founder Captain Howey, Gladys is the bar car providing snacks and both soft and alcoholic drinks. When the line celebrated its 75th anniversary in 2002 RHDR released their own Celebration Steam Ale.

Teak luggage carriage
This is one of the teak carriages which are being refurbished as part of an
ongoing programme, shown here at St Mary's Bay.

Fame at last
The facial expression of the child in the centre of this picture says so much: eagerness to get under way, a touch of uncertainty about what the experience will be like, and a slightly stifled smile into the camera that suggests he's not sure whether this photograph is going to bring him his fifteen minutes of fame or not.

111

No.10 Doctor Syn

No bright paint job here, I'm afraid. Doctor Syn's running gear is looking decidedly well-used,
but with a bit of light and different framing (*opposite*) she doesn't look quite so time-worn.

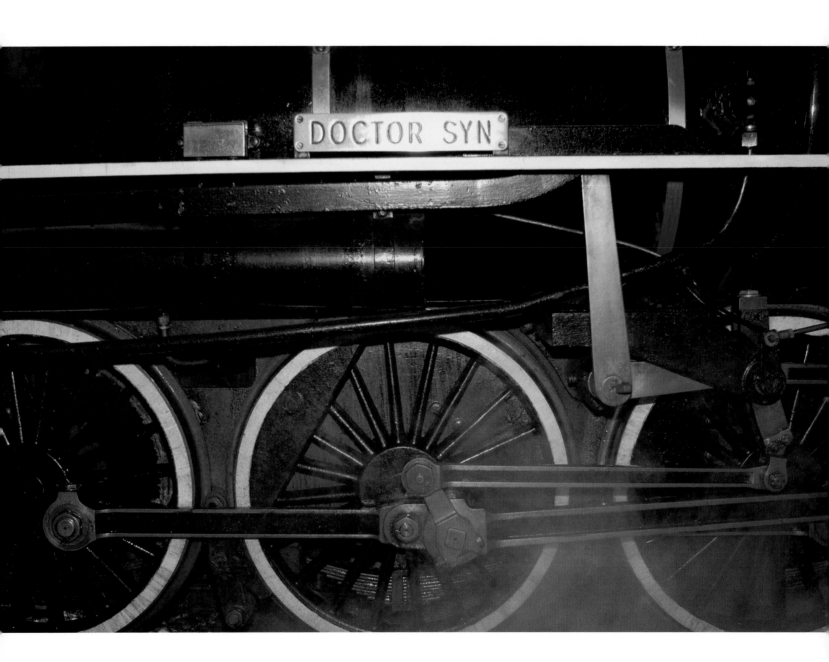

113

Coal yard, New Romney
No.7 Typhoon, having loaded up with
fuel, backs out of the coal yard as the
morning sun breaks through
the trees. This is one of the first
jobs of the day for every driver.

Distinguishing detail
The white lamps mounted on the front of No.6 Samson
serve to distinguish it from other engines.

Steam makes all the difference
Without the steam this shot wouldn't work half so well. Getting the exposure right is critical so as to preserve some detail within the clouds of steam and not allow it to be reduced to a white mass with no depth to it.

Opposite: No.9 Winston Churchill at Dymchurch Station
Tightly cropped images of the locomotives themselves are always useful but it is also good to place the subject in context as what we refer to as an 'establishing shot'.

Tight fit
Most of us, at one time or
another, complain about our
working conditions, but with
it being even smaller than the rest
of RHDR's locos the cab on
No.4 The Bug is an even
tighter squeeze.

No.11 Black Prince entering New Romney Station

Black Prince is unusual in not having its number emblazoned on its buffer bar. I couldn't discover the reason for this but it does make identification easier.

119

Young and old alike
One of the great surprises in the preparation of this book was the wide age
range of those who demonstrated real enthusiasm for the locomotives.

Opposite: Tunnel at New Romney
The road from New Romney to the beach passes over the line
on the Dungeness side of New Romney Station. By standing at the
end of the platform it is possible to shoot beneath the low footbridge
as trains emerge from the tunnel.

Vantage point
No.9 Winston Churchill passing southbound beneath the road bridge adjacent to Romney Marsh Visitor Centre, half a mile outside New Romney. During peak season there's only a brief gap between trains running in both directions at this point.

Capturing the unusual

Most enthusiasts opt to take photos of the locos looking their best but occasionally opportunities arise for an unusual treatment. Here the Winston Churchill is smothered by blankets outside the sheds.

No.10 Doctor Syn

These two images are part of a series taken over several minutes while Doctor Syn was taking on water.
What I love about the whole series is the way the driver gradually emerges in greater and greater detail.

New Romney workshops
The running gear of No.4 The Bug is quite tiny compared with that of the steam locomotives.

Spanner in the works

Or, more accurately, in the workshops. In an age when our cars go into garages to be have their computer chips assessed by mechanics who have had to learn computer skills in order to carry out repairs, it was pleasing to find good old chrome vanadium spanners in regular use in the workshops.

Composition

It's interesting to play with composition with detail shots like these. The first gives a distinct feeling of movement, despite being shot standing still, whereas the right-angles in the second image create a very solid and stationary feel to the same subject.

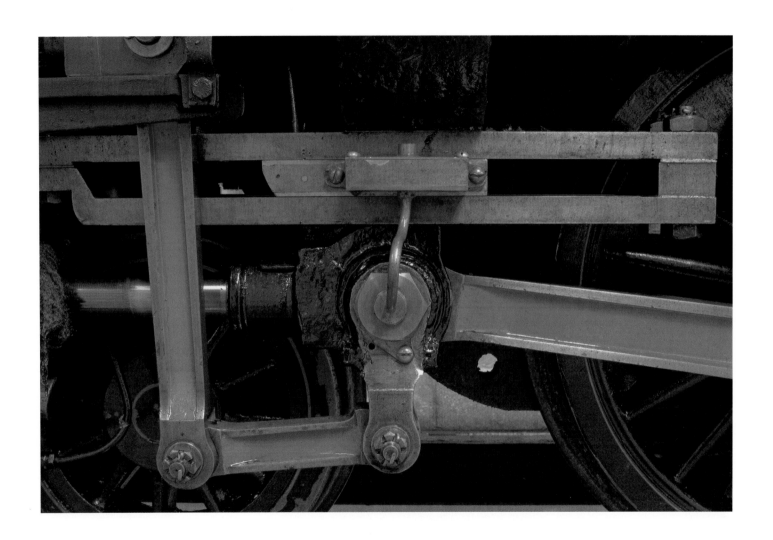

Convergence
The tracks, the white lines along the platform edges, and the straight lines of the carriage, tender and loco draw the eye into this atmospheric image.

Signalman

Pictured here is the signalman at New Romney who also operates the points immediately outside the signal box.

Familiar landmarks

While New Romney provides the easiest location at which to photograph a wide variety of RHDR subjects, it is hard to avoid this set of signals and the signal box in the background!

Opposite: Warp speed

This stretch of line between Dymchurch and Hythe runs across open countryside. It also has several level crossings and a couple of wooden bridges which are often used by photographers as foreground. This is a section of the line on which drivers can go to full throttle, normally achieving about 25mph.

No.8 Hurricane detail
It's not often that you'll have the chance to photograph your subjects with their clothes off, so to speak. However, a pre-arranged visit to the New Romney workshops found Hurricane completely stripped for a rebuild, with opportunities for some unusual close-ups.

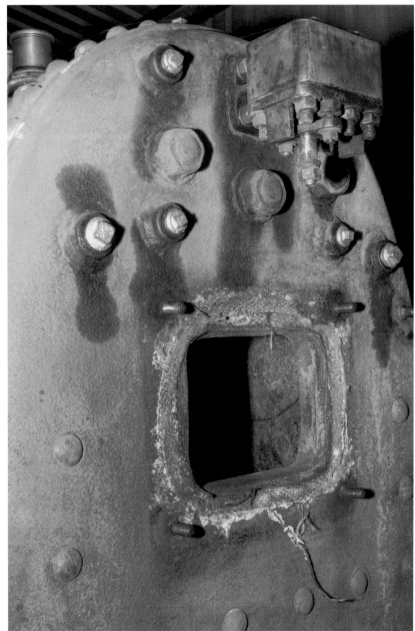

No.4 The Bug

During my visits I remember talking with one lady who had travelled along the line but had not had a close look inside one of the cabs. She was under the impression that all the controls were digital. Er, not exactly!

Four star service
A simple detail shot but I like the lighting in contrast to the matt black of the background.

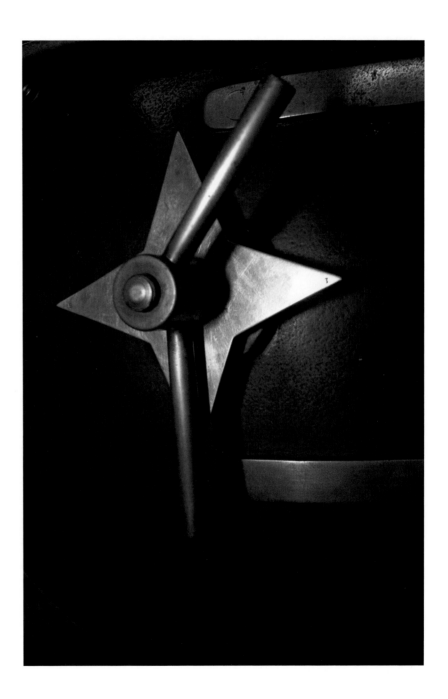

Model railway
Although most of the exhibition at New Romney is given over to the extensive
working model railway, there are other exhibits which give pleasure too.

No.7 Typhoon driven by Mike Jacques
When viewed from a distance the scale of these locomotives isn't
as obvious as when you get up close. Driver Mike Jacques is shown
here at Dungeness, his nameplate proudly displayed in the cab into
which he has to squeeze.

Pampas grass at New Romney

It's not easy to find interesting backgrounds along the line,
especially as so much of it runs along the bottom of people's
gardens, so things like this clump of pampas grass are a good
opportunity to introduce a little variety.

Opposite: No.2 Northern Chief at New Romney

This is one of the classic shots of New Romney Station, taken
while No.2 Northern Chief is waiting to depart on the northern
half of the line to Hythe. When the RHDR first opened this was
as far as the trains from Hythe could go before needing
to turn around and begin the return journey.

Letting off steam
The importance of including steam in your photos is clearly shown here. This shot of No.6 Samson's distinctive
white lamps and red buffer bar benefits from the steam which surrounds the front of the loco.

The same is true of this image, also of Samson, but the diagonal line made by the jet of steam creates a little more drama and even a suggestion of backward movement.

Countdown

It seems fitting to end this book with an image which conveys a touch of mystery, amid clouds of steam, and of a locomotive which has served the RHDR so well over the years that it really is counting the days to retirement.